BLOODLETTING IN MINOR SCALES
[*A CANVAS IN ARMS.*]

Bloodletting in Minor Scales [*A Canvas in Arms.*]
© 2014 Justin Limoli

Published by Plays Inverse Press
Pittsburgh, PA
www.playsinverse.com

Early versions of some of these scenes appeared previously in *Columbia Poetry Review.* Thank you to the editors.

ISBN 13: 978-0-9914183-1-2

First Printing: December 2014
Cover art and design by David Watt
Page design by Tyler Crumrine
Printed in the U.S.A.

PLAYS
INVERSE

BLOODLETTING IN MINOR SCALES
[*A CANVAS IN ARMS.*]
JUSTIN LIMOLI

PLAYS INVERSE PRESS
PITTSBURGH, PA

2014

To Dana and Ramona,
who stand and listen to this
unfolding, knowing
what I mean to say.

ACT I: BLOODLETTING IN MINOR SCALES

Epigraph:

Mental Ward: [Opens all seeds caked in skin.]
Inside me there are words
constricting the skinned
lips of knives to the prayer
holdings of syntax.

To my mother who is brought back.

[*Justin* reads to *The Audience* in place of *Pantoum*.]

This is the first line that plucks the stringed notes of my mother's body.
This is the first line that calls her into being.
This is the first line that disassembles the inner verse of blood.
This line commits suicide, leaking into folded skin, becoming grief.

My mother is botched, becoming the first line to admit existing.
My mother is insufficiently dead, and consequently the line gets treated.
My lines commit themselves to memory, folding grief into language,
becoming my mother, the first line I cannot finish.

She is insufficiently dead: a postmortem maternity ward
that is brought back as the remains of my moving mother.
The remnant body of my first line gives birth to the second line,
attempting the remaking of suicide, spilling my mother.

She moves within this line, drawing her remains in blood,
immersed in the shaping of her death, veins and tongues spilled
and then the first line attempts a re-emerging with the lisping of knives
forming vowels that cut my self-inflicted mother to breath.

Her tongue spills her shapeless bones into an obsession with chords
and dissonant immersions of soundless bleeding and snapped skin.
These syllables I call to her living body are now slit into an opening
that exposes the unfleshed resuscitation of my mother's deepest red.

My mother's snapped skin chimes with a non-scarring of words,
Justin, you might not forgive me, heard through a resuscitation of hearts.
The reimagining of my mother as a condensed death of a line—
the last line that plucks away at my mother's body.

Character List:

Character List: (Other aliases include *Dramatis Personae* and, more commonly, *Persona Non Grata*.) *Character List* is brought to *Stage* on the back of the wood-split shoulders of *Atlas*, who is now just *Compass* with age. *Character List*, constantly gorging on minor characters, wreathed and spoon-fed, is an overflowing slow progression, an abundance of otherwise-movement pressing into *Atlas's* forgotten shoulders, humming the entire time to the intake of *Atlas's* breath.

Stage Fright: *Stage Fright* encompasses all characters in certain moments of remorse, but *Remorse* is constantly out of character. By the end of the play, *Stage Fright* will take root on the great Pedestal of Laurels, flower, and then spoil, but remain to conclude his ending as the most articulate to blemish.

Orchestra Pit: A canopy of fruit interlaced with the awakening of strings. *The Narrator*, who shall remain motionless until the sound of catharsis is required, conducts *Orchestra Pit*. *Orchestra Pit* is covered in body hair, consuming the children of *Odysseus* but, like all Greek myths, the children escape from splitting.

Chair 1:   Directs the currents of the play while remaining seated and eating tarot cards. *Chair 1's* face is embalmed so as to ward off the intentions of *Narrative*. It is also rumored that *Chair 1* is a byproduct of *Character List*.

Chair 2:   Accumulates *Rigor Mortis* as an act of penance. Invokes the turning point, but smothers the other solvents. *Chair 2* is not *Chair 1*, but the reverse cannot be said.

In Medias Res: See *Mombo*.

Act 3:   *Act 3* has greater value than *Act 1* and *Act 2*. *Act 3* is intrinsically beautiful, but this cannot be written without loss. Sucking on lemons for pitfalls, *Act 3* is seduced by a demi-god that turns out to be *Chair 1*. It must be noted that this was all unscripted.

Mombo: She is the grandmother of *The Narrator* and this is an ending. *Age* is the only character to remember the origin of her familiar name, but this character is unremembered, planting roots inside *Character List*.

Mom: *Mom* spends her time dying on stage. Her most successful scenes are those that require blood loss and dramatic resuscitation. *Mom* embodies the interrogation of forgiveness, but this is a lesser creature formed and then given to *Character List*.

Dad: See *Unspoken Poem*.

Justin: A ghostly figure that haunts the ongoing existence of the play. As a narrator, he is a ghost; as a ghost, he is silked in skin. He attempts to shroud, unbinding *Narrative* with superstitious *Poetry*, disfiguring the chaining of words, acknowledging that he is the ghost of *Narration*. But *Narration* must hold truth, and believe that it can affix itself to *Poetry* without condensation, or, a more honest word choice, dilution. What *Justin* tries to say, he does through *Poetry*, hoping that there is a *Narrative*, and that the two are not mutually exclusive. But they are mutually exclusive. *Poetry* upholds the value of sound and image, tries to sound like *Poetry*, acclimated to abstract dissonances, whereas *Narrative* is subjective to *Poetry*. But *Justin* is coded in *Poetry*, not to be confused with 'coda', which is more of a repetitive occurrence than anatomical. For the last time in *Character List*, *Justin* attempts a ghostly mothering of *Poetry*, and is successful in his inclusion of self-reflexive characters.

Poetry: See *Femme Fatale* without the corset of words.

Self-Reflexive: Un-see *Justin*.

Narrative: Dons the Grecian mask of *Poetry*.

Stage: *Stage* embodies the weight of judgment that all great epics disfigure for closure.

Beginning

[*Justin*, dressed in a bloodletting tuxedo and surgical mask, taps a floating *Cadaver* with a conductor's baton. His cheeks are swollen tungsten red, eyes quivering with spit, his nose quietly undoing its falsetto interruptions. *The Moment to Begin*, veiled in a white shore, addresses *Justin*, singing to stop. *Baton* steps over *Justin*, drifting toward *Sound*. *Sound* takes this moment, possessing *Cadaver* with a key in the process. *Cadaver* moves, sinking towards an embrace with the ground. *Baton* sprouts a wilting *Timpani*, thumping until still. *Sound* is quiet.

Unmoved, *Cadaver* places *Baton* in its mouth, playing spoiled intervals over *Justin*, a slowly disquiet duet. The air hardens as *Sound* breathes again. *Cadaver*, now the darkening shore sweeping with sinking steps, continues its improvised movement to a stop, ingests its instrument, and with a brushstroke becomes *Stage*. *Sound* ingests its phantoms, waiting while *Justin* continues to hold on to the duet, wringing the droplets. In the painted background, *Stage* skins its sheet music, sprouting its naked curtains…

After many years of *Stage* growing into shape, *Mom* runs onto *Stage* panting, reciting words to collect her sounds, consequently phantoms. *Justin*, with a full collage of faults, becomes many, all singing to stop.]

Mom: I am at fault for this.

[*Mom* impales her left wrist with a swooning cleaver, a chandelier of *Blood* enters through her, and *Justin* is left. He plants his unsoiled tongue into his chest, so that it may pollinate with his heart. *Mom* is dragged offstage and thrown into the inner ribs of *Mental Ward* to recuperate.]

Justin: [Eyes holding back the image.] My mother—

Blood: I am Blood, the
bleeding finite.

Justin: Is this the beginning?

Blood: [Plucks *Justin's* left iris.] Yes, and all beginnings need victims.

Justin: My mother just cut—

Blood: Yes, I saw. Now the play can get started.

Justin: This is cruel.

Blood: No, this is narration. [Shapes *Justin's* remaining sight into a calloused blade. *Blood* slits the entire length of *Justin's* torso.] There, you've been branded as The Narrator.

Justin: [Ignores his intimate spilling.] I didn't want this.

Blood: You have a story to tell, so here are your stage and canvas. [Lops an ear off *Justin* and coddles the earlobe with whispers.] Narrate.

[*Mom* reconfigures her inner dialogue.]

Mom: Hello?

Justin: I didn't want this.

Blood: [Licking the scent of earlobes.] Narrate!

Justin: [In a syncopated off-meter.]
               My name is Justin
               and my mother
               slit her wrist
               with a cleaver

[Stage Theory 1]

[*Mental Ward* opens to reveal]:

Schrödinger's Cat[1]:   A thought experiment, sometimes described as a devised paradox. It illustrates what the audience sees as the problem of everyday objects—
> [a bowl of milk,
> dead dialogue flapping on the floor,
> flat cooing over sleep,
> the audience crawling out of the litter box,
> still a cat,
> Schrödinger,
> a devised scheme,
> the newly minted term,
> his alternate cat,
> everyday,
> no remorse for dead things]—

resulting in a dead-and-alive cat contradiction with common sense depending on an earlier random event in a box.

---

[1] Coined the term "entanglement."

Suicide's **Monologue** [*Turning Point*]

Enter *Suicide*.[2]

[*Suicide* is visibly an opal bruising: blemishing crimson, blue contortions, limbs cracking beneath bone, possibly green somewhere. Hunched over, there is a regal impatience to *Suicide*, quietly smoking a stick of gum, carving the floor with an ivory cane. Most of *The Audience* is in hibernation. *Justin* is caught off-guard, intently watching this new character.]

Suicide: My name is Suicide, and this is a greeting. My name is Suicide repeatedly. My suicide was a naming, and I am here to tell you something. My name in robes is Suicide. I stole a color with a naming. In brush strokes, there is a swifting breath of suicide. You might be wondering why this is all relevant? I can assure you that my name is Suicide and there is relevance in brush strokes. A happening will occur, but I am not omnipotent. I am Suicide, and for this act, that means everything.

[Waits for *Applause*, but commits
The Audience to a noose. A fog
engulfs the curtains in sage.
There are stars drowning underneath
the canvas: a skinning
embroidery. The canvas begins
to gurgle in the throes of shape
(a molded blood orange). The fleshed
orange is worn in folds. *The Audience*
awakens and accumulates. They follow
Suicide offstage.]

---

[2] Note to actor in role of *Suicide*: The rest of the play hinges on the success of *Suicide*.

Godot **Enters through a Body of Curtains**

Enter *Godot* to an empty *Audience.*

Godot: Hello?

Stage: [No response.]

Godot: [The first introduction of light binds to *Foresight.*]
      Hello? Can somebody tell me what my line is? Hello?

[He looks at his watch. An impatient *Watch* melts. *Watch* melts from waiting. *Watch* cuts its intent of numbers. *Godot* and his watch melt. There is a time that needs to be 12:00. No response. No saying, "Hello, my name is Godot and thus extinguishing the impulse to wait." *Godot* and his watch, "What is my line again?" continue to wait. *The Audience* folds *Godot* into *Watch* telling time. *Godot* "Hello" and his watch. The scarring of time into *Godot* festers a ticking *Watch* and you will be [No response.] too. *Godot* and his consumption of watches. Hello? Hello? "I can't really hear what he's saying, like it's melting," and no *Godot* to strip into units of beating seconds. *Godot* breathes in, and out comes across *Time,* all arms and legs. *Godot* continues to an empty *Audience.* Wait. Wait. *Watch,* a 'no please' response, I beg [stop] of you. Can somebody tell me what my line is again? *Godot* looks at his and everything else together. Wait, no don't tell me. "Is he okay?" Foot tapping, arms crossed waiting name. *Godot.* What time is it, and why is it so important? Last time I checked, it was 12:00. To find fault in time. To read into time's inaccuracies and salty dilemmas. Wait. Twelve hours ago, what was I doing? *Godot* winds up with a watch correctly ticking away with "Hello." The sun rises and sinks, rises and sinks, with *Watch* holding up a tied-down *Time* smiling. An empty "Hello" greets this sinking feeling. *Godot,* what am I supposed to say? Besides "Wait." An empty line. *Godot* stares at a blank *Watch.* Wait. *Godot* continues to act surprised, waiting for 12:00 and its ticking.]

Enter *Mental Ward* carrying a disfigured *12:00.*

Mental Ward: No, not yet.

Somewhere offstage[3] [A Manifesto in Song]

Mom: [Singing.]

My suicide, with the corralled hair
My suicide, with the flames in the attic
My suicide, with the leaking jade
My suicide, with the skinned locket
My suicide, as a mercury-steeled secret
My suicide, with the smile-laced ivy
My suicide, as the omega blossom
My suicide, the numbers holding turquoise
My suicide, with the lips of a teething chord
My suicide, with the smile of a stabbed host
My suicide, the eyelash of rubbed saffron
My suicide, the beechnut fountain
My suicide, coping with Shakespeare
My suicide, desire's ink-blotted thighs
My suicide, with the flaring legs
My suicide, clockwork telling
My suicide, initials in feet
My suicide, with breasts of an ambered ruby
My suicide, the fleeing vertical bird
My suicide, quicksilver in descent
My suicide, unpearled open
My suicide, inside the soured rose bed
My suicide, armed in naked pivots of form
My suicide, the pendulum swing of eyelids
My suicide, with eyes of water always under the axe
My suicide, unstitched buttons on the swan's back

---

[3] For *André Breton.*

Mental Ward's **Monologue**

[*Mental Ward* is rolled onto *Stage*, duct-taped to a straitjacket crowned in thorns, and opens. Inside, the body reveals castrated floral patterns of silent skin, splitting the wrist's contorted tongues.]

Mental Ward:

1. Depict *my stillness to suicide,*
as a repeated action.

2. [*my stillness to suicide.*]

3. Count each cymbaled
second with the same face,
passing over
lavender, passing over
a sleepless panic, passing over
the little sounds clanging
inside quiet.

4. Distort the sound of memory.

5. Remember: I want to bear
you within this
structural body.

6. [a missing response.]

7. Recite your body
to its small universe
of fluids

8. Write: *It's more like sifting when you
try to hold it.*

9. Your breath is leaving without you.

Justin's **Monologue**

Justin (*as a splitting*):

A dialogue between fingers but singular deaths
underneath nail beds. Momentary catharsis, and
you're bleeding. How many times? How many
of us watching? A spoonful solidifying into
each moment lapsing. My line breaks, my
repetitions, my thoughts, my list of things
to do. I can't. I don't think I'm ready for poetry.
I can't. Mom, you are still dying. Mom, I think
I am not sorry. Mom, I can't stop apologizing.
I don't know what I did, but is this even right?
Mom, my lines are breaking, and this isn't the
first time. There wasn't a dialogue in your fingers.
I eat nail beds and you sleep under the mantra of
you lashing out in fluids. Was there a time of scents?
What color? Mom, this isn't the first time.
I write, I write, and I am speaking, but these words
suffer from nail beds. But I am bleeding. May I?

[*He does.*]

Maternal Red Blossoms Petalled

[*Justin* reads to *Pantoum* in a dialect foreign to *Stage*.]

Blossoms where your wrists were—an epigraph,
and then another slated with cracks your petals show.
My mother, she... I did not watch, I didn't, but I dream about it.
Mother, this is the fourth line, the one that won't be repeated.

An epigraph sounds out its missing parts to this petalless quiet.
Should I confess that I wanted to be there?
Mother, what was the fourth line is now the third line of this stanza.
Cut the sign of the cross into your wrists, and after, kneel.

Should I confess to your wrists that I have nothing to say?
I have nothing to say, and yet I keep writing, and calling you mother.
And you cross yourself with your wrists, treading on obsession.
Mother, this voice of mine is foreign and bleeding.

I am tired of calling to you in my poems,
and death is a slitting obsession of you dying over and over.
But my mother is dying on the hardwood floor,
the repetition of incisions frantic, fading, and through your fingers.

Here—in this line, I give you the death of me not knowing.
I slipped through your veins, the ones that nourish, yours.
My repetitions are not the same, and you didn't have to tell me,
but that's not true, like my blue veins within the deepest of colors hiding.

Slipping implicates depth, and the gravity within your skin is related,
but what happened? And I am repeating myself, which I sometimes do,
lying to tell only myself, "She didn't mean to, she didn't mean to, etc."
But she did, and I keep it, and it's so sad that you lived.

There was too much to say, and you spilled choices
in our kitchen, leaving my voice a foreign thing that my atoms carry
with the same mass and quantity, so I haven't changed in numbers.
But you did, as I witnessed the depth of your red's repetitions.

[Stage Theory 2]

[*Mental Ward* opens to reveal]:

Buckminsterfullerene[4]:   (lovingly called *Buckyball*) A lost
character not found in spherical fullerenes with the formula for
quantifiable stage direction. *Bucky* has a curtain-like ring structure or,
with each step, a "Truncated Icosahedral Curtain Closing," which acts
to resemble twenty hexagons and twelve pentagrams with a carbon
character molding at each vertex bond. While miscast as *Micro-Fullerene
#4* in "Bucky Takes a Hit," he stirred the largest applause to exhibit
wave-particle duality in deep space in the form of a play.

---

[4] Revisit *Stage Entanglement*.

Mother, as a Swelling Word

[An unidentified *Body of Forgotten Characters* rises from the balcony.
The following words bear the markings of a throat undergoing violence
dedicated to the self.]

Ashes between the two strokes
of cognizance. You awake
with webbings around your lowest parts
of arms dangling. The worst part knowing
you meant it in full flesh. [Enter *Aroma of Dangling.*]
My mourning, a process of decalcifying
my marrow alone. My breathing buried in
"we have the same shade of burning."
[Enter *What We Share*, the same breath
my fingers touch.]

But I was taken out of your context—
a responsive movement;
within you, a directional posture.
[Enter *Fingers* carrying *Arms* off
to sleep in a forest.]

These are words forever paused
or in a state of shadings. [Enter
an acknowledgment from two parties
that something happened
here.] Can this language
convey such a swelling
word? I am unsure, but
you are no longer withheld.

The formula of our genes kept afloat below suffocation by
my fingers coursing from acknowledging
the dead: an act of punctuation. [Enter *the burial site*
where I placed my breaking actions and heavy movements.]

An unwinding between
you and your thoughts,
the sound of that unwanted
panting, the question,
at some point,
did your body shrivel?

[Stage Theory 3]

[*Mental Ward* opens to reveal]:

Interpretation Universe: This treatment
[*Mom,* I am
sorry.] focuses on
explaining behavior
from the perspective
of *Interpretation,*

in which

a phenomenon
can be viewed
in one way
or in another,
but not in both
simultaneously.

I can't give this a name.

[*Justin* is placed in an oven where he is greeted by two chairs. *Chair 1* is comprised of oyster shells, *Chair 2* vomits nacre. The remainder of the scene is unscripted. *Chair 1* swallows *Justin* to a place outside of the oven. *Chair 2* is dying, choking on pearls.[5] *Chair 1* is an exoskeleton of questions. Angry, *Chair 2* grabs a member of *The Audience*, cracks the wrists, and swallows the marrow (more pearls). *Justin* vomits the oven. *Chair 1* grows impatient and vomits the characters onto the scene's birthplace: *Stage*. He gives the characters time to nourish. *Chair 1* crosses his legs and waits (engulfed in the mouth of *Chair 2*).]

Chair 1:   [Folding over the edges of its legs, becoming a silted chair-swan.] In what room do you imagine yourself as a dream?

Justin: [After *Moments* passes.] What a stupid question.

Chair 1:   [Expressing *Blank*.] I don't know what to say.

Justin: [Writes something down.] I am a room of dreams. I dream of rooms. I room myself in dreams. Why? Do I look like I dream? I tend not to imagine myself in any form other than the present. I can't sleep, room or otherwise, so I dream, presently sleeping off the dream. But I want to.

Chair 1:   [*Momentum* stops to listen.] When did you last think about death?

Justin: I died when I thought about dreams. I can't hold on to this death though. There is copper in it. There is water within the copper. But within that, there is metal and me dreaming within a small room with a campfire dangling in the middle of my chest. But within my chest there is me dreaming. Though, I sometimes count the breaths of my father.

---

[5] Note to *Chair 2*: Death is the potential of pearls.

Chair 1:	How many breaths does your father hold?
Justin:	I don't imagine this. I think of my mother a lot, not my father. My mother is sleeping and I am thinking in terms of her geography, and the circumference of her bleeding. [Pauses.] And now I have planted geography and bleeding inside my mother's sleeping body. [*Chair 1* continues improving his swan.] I don't want to do this anymore. [*Justin* gets up, but after taking the initial steps of flight, finds himself again in a chair facing a swan-diving *Chair 1*.] My father breathes, and grows older, but he is not a safe place. His breaths are acknowledgments of my mother. He grows in breaths. He grows, and I am left as my father, but my mother is still killing herself. She kills herself holding my breath, so I ask my father still breathing his age: how many breaths in a breath? How many more can I blame? When should I stop counting?
Chair 1:	When was the last time you felt yourself adding tenses?
Justin:	I fold myself in tenses: trying to contort finer shadows into shapes I can't hold faces to. I know this is wrong, but what I have to hold is my father, and I felt along these tenses of myself. My wrists express pulse tenses, and I don't know how to tell you this.
Chair 1:	[Chewing on pearls, savoring their salt.] How do you consume?
Justin:	[Finds a feather instead of a loose hair in his mouth. There is a perfumed note tied to the feather inscribed by *Chair 1*, but it is quickly discarded by swallowing.] I consume using the pronoun "I" and the present tense of "consume," but secretly, there is mourning in my consumption. I consume through tubes, dilators, and stitching. In my chest you will find consumption. When I was a child, I grew through this, consuming the sun. The sun consumes, and it too is mourning. It will die by consumption, becoming a mourning figure, a literate device for self that I will plant in a dream.

Chair 1:   [Looks into *Justin's* eyes finding a handful of feathers stemming.] Was there a purpose in your mother's suffering?

Justin: [The organ chord holding *Justin* to this oven setting snaps. He tries to callous again.] Was there a purpose in your mother's suffering?

Chair 1:   [Holds *Justin's* musical lingering.] Was there a purpose in your mother's suffering?

Justin: [Dissolves everything that led up to this moment.] Was there a purpose in your mother's suffering?

Chair 1:   [Lies on top of the decayed *Audience*, orchestrating.] Was there a purpose in your mother's suffering?

Justin: [Discovers no footing.] Was there a purpose in your mother's suffering?

Chair 1:   [Embodies the question.] Was there a purpose in your mother's suffering?

Justin: [Embodies the response.] She broke me into decimals.

[*Stage* nods and leaves.]

Suicide* repeats *Ulysses

[*Justin* dangles from the limbs of *The Last Scene*, watching again. *The Last Scene* is composed decomposing, fading out to a darker pitch, slipping through the stage direction, leaving a ringing behind. *Molly Bloom* approaches as the *Femme Fatale*, and dons *Premonition*. *Premonition* is blood-soaked. *Justin* is a fingerprint in language. *Molly Bloom* begins the dialogue in a muted corner. For what it's worth, *I'm Sorry* is misplaced.]

Molly Bloom: [Assertively *Molly Bloom*.] Yes.

Premonition: This doesn't bode well.

Molly Bloom: Yes, I said.

I'm Sorry: [Needing to shave.] Oh no!

Molly Bloom: [Resembling the *Penultimate Molly Bloom*.] Yes, I said, "Yes."

[*Justin* holds a misplaced *Heart* but allows it to thorn.]

Molly Bloom: [To *Heart*.] Hello, and you are?

Heart: I am, yes, I am.

I'm Sorry: [Finds himself breaking a surface.] You've thorned.

Heart: [To *Justin*.] Let go, please, you're breaking.

[*Justin's Grip* tightens.]

Heart: [Muffled.] In other meters of speech, I can't breathe.

[*Heart's* left side deflates.]

I'm Sorry: This can't be right. [His facial hair pollinates.] No, no, no, this can't be right.

Molly Bloom: "Yes" is an inadequate ending.

[*Justin* plunges a fountain pen into *Heart*. *Heart* is now an inked setting with cursive.]

Heart: [To *Justin*.] You clearly are not very good at conversing with hearts.

Molly Bloom: Why, is it hard?

Justin: [Writes.] I'm not very good with things buried in my chest.

Heart: Correct! As it should be, my sniveling lemon drop! This is post-Shakespearean. The heart should not be spoken to directly. Speak to me, but never about me. But always indirectly, or else you run the risk of—oh what's the term? It's French. I can assure you it's French. [There is a hoard of circles approaching stage left.]

Molly Bloom: [Yes.] Stephen Dedalus?

I'm Sorry: [Rotates an impossible figure.] Nihilism?

Cliché: [Descends from the ceiling to introduce a voice that violets.] I don't know either. [Splat! Silent.]

Heart: [Finds *Cliché* now ripening in amniotic fluid.] I need to disolve myself of this situation [But remains as a solvent.].

Justin: My mom, she—[With another pen, slashes his wrists. He feeds *Blood* to *Heart*, choking on the underwords.]

Molly Bloom: [Showering in linens.] Yes.

I'm Sorry: [*Intimate* parts *Molly*.] Yes.

Heart: [Quietly deafened through *Crescendo*.] Please, stop! Enough!

Justin: My mom, she—[Repeat.]

Heart: [Still under a practiced *Pianissimo*.] Yes, I understand. But what do you want me to do?

[*Justin* takes his wrist and self-consumes. After another act of *Nourishment*, *Justin* feeds *Heart* to *Stage* and waits.]

Stage: Are you sure?

[*Justin* sprinkles *Stage* with *Spit* from a basket. There is fermentation within *Stage*. *Justin* waits and a twisting dissonance is heard. *The Audience* applauds, clustering in cardamom. *Blood* screams melodically, while *Molly Bloom* and *I'm Sorry* are glimpsed drowning in linens.]

[*Justin* is a statue of swirling yellows. *Mother* peels herself out of *Stage*. *The Audience* is stab-counting amongst themselves. *Mother* stops *Justin's* bleeding. *Justin* gives her his tongue.]

Mother: Justin, did you do this?

[*Justin* wraps himself in *Curtains*.]

Mother: [Wipes away his creasing mouth.] Did you do this?

[*Justin* wraps himself in *Dialogue*.]

Mother: [Wipes away the space left.] Did you do this?

Justin: How else can I convey what you did without a tongue?

[Stage Theory 4]

[*Mental Ward* opens to reveal]:

Coherent Light: Light waves that are
in phase [6]
containing
several distinct
scenes, which are limit
cases that never occur
in reality but allow
an understanding.

---

[6] Synchronized atonal collision.

Pre-I.12: *Dialogue's* Monologue (What Prefaces the Continuing)

[*Dialogue* is a setting after awakening from a dreamscape. He checks the flight of birds within and divines that he must leave a note.]

Dialogue: [Verbed tense.]

Dear Audience,

A dialogue is meant to conceive what I cannot
say. I cannot say (*repeated*) because I am
simply an experimentation of language.
[Unstitches his mouth to prove it.]
I am not supposed to include the events
of the cutting. [*Thimble* becomes *Lemon*.] But
what I can say is that I tried not to conceive
the limbs of my mother and splay them
into a word, but a depiction
is the death of limbs.

Audience, I am sorry. I wasn't meant
for language. [*Lemon* is coaxed into *Mother*.]
I wasn't meant to be Dialogue, but now I am
a setting where the limbs address
dialogue and whether death should occur once
the decision to splice occurs.

My mother spliced language, which is in essence
the olfactory of poetry. [*Mother* appears
as a lemoned thimble until *Dialogue*
is coarsely ground.] But there was an important moment
I am forgetting to mention. I believe I am supposed to declare
something. [*Dialogue* undergoes strangulation by the
lip-stitching.]

[Writing through fits of diction.] Audience, I am sorry
(*repeated*), but poetry does not suit the narrative and I am
dying in letters. [There is a *Thimble* before death, and after,
only death.]

Illiterate,
Dialogue

Between Act I.12 [Enter the Anti-Narrator]

Enter Antagonist.

Antagonist: [Fights through the reflections of pointed fingers.] It seems that this is my fault. But I've only just appeared in the play. This is troubling. But what have I done? [Begins to breathe verbatim, but ultimately rolls himself offstage {left}.]

There is an Off-Moment somewhere.

[He begins slashing away at *The Audience. The Audience* accumulates and forms a scowl. He continues to dance through corpses, and considers the action fraternal. (This will become important, and then in hindsight, a scene in remission.) He dons *The Audience*, recognizes his lineage (half-Italian), and departs for *The Climax*.]

Enter The 100 years of Cent'anni ⁷ from a departed field.

---

[7] Where the *Antagonist* sings and shrouds, practices his 100 years, singing away from all fields, *Cent'anni* and its meaning to all who come to pass, singing dearly departed fields, deserted songs shrouding offstage in a half-Italian towards the *Antagonist's* monologue, where the fermented *Cent'anni* fields in difficult language of this losing phrase, the play's departed forming around the *Antagonist* singing this whole time from another, and out comes a departed song of fields where no one slashes away the language, *Meaning as Listening*, the heritage of the *Antagonist* opens, spoiling the surprise of singing *Cent'anni*, wanting *may you live* to mean something longer in grieving, never singing in the first place, slender but practicing what has been done with departed fruit, meaning fruit only once, and not the *Antagonist*, who is half-Italian, half-listening to this song, while the rest open fields departed, rolling stage left, dancing in hindsight, needing to be Anti-*Cent'anni*, but the *Antagonist* considers the word after seeking his own nourishment, and leaves *Cent'anni* curdled, singing *may you live 100 years*, and planted in a departed field.

Act I.12: The Death of *Dialogue*

[After feeding on the remnants of the newest generation of *The Audience*, *Antagonist* is caught fragmenting *Dialogue*. This is not a nativity scene, but absolution. *Justin* watches from a spurting growth of distance.]

Dialogue: [The mouth forms shapes.]

Antagonist: Still not going to say anything? [Peels back *Dialogue's* knees.]

Dialogue: [The air shimmers between the teeth.]

Antagonist: I believe there was never really any point in creating you. [*Dialogue* is met with a hammer.]

Dialogue: [The air forms the mouth. The teeth bear what shimmers.]

Antagonist: I needed you to say *something*! [Further feelings are conveyed through violent means and/or methods of your pleasure.]

Dialogue: [At a certain point, the brain forgets about the mouth and teeth.]

Antagonist: A functioning climax must establish emotional catharsis in some form. [Noticeably not *Catharsis*, nor *Climax*.] I am not the catharsis, but I want to be. [Attempts *Catharsis*, but softly stokes an undoing.] No, no, I was not created to shape Catharsis.

Dialogue: [Retraces the pieces of the self.]

Antagonist: I can't help but think her leaving her wrists wrapped in paper was my fault. But that's the thing with suicide; ultimately everyone feels responsible.

Fade-in to unearned *Catharsis*.

I didn't mean to tell you this. There was probably some other way to reveal it. Regardless, I still think this is true. [Looks over at *Dialogue*.] Won't you say something?

Enter *You* escaping.

You: What are you doing to Dialogue?

Antagonist: What is deserved.

You: But you did this.

Antagonist: I did what was in character, but Dialogue was out of character. He didn't do anything.

You: So this is acceptable? [*You* looks at *Dialogue*.]

Dialogue: [Whimpering condemns the mouth to engage with the brain.]

Antagonist: See? He doesn't do anything!

You: Is he illiterate?

Antagonist: Ask him.

You: [To *Dialogue*.] Why don't you speak?

Dialogue: [Descends down the steps leading up to the birth of *Dialogue*.]

Antagonist: [To *Dialogue*.] May I remind you that you are mine to commit! [Plunges what commits *Dialogue* to memory.]

You:	Stop! Please!
Antagonist:	Please?
You:	Yes, please.

Enter *Pause* and *Self-Reflection*.

Antagonist:	I drove her to it.
You:	Drove whom to what?
Antagonist:	My mother she… [Spoiling digests the pause.] Where did I put my knife?
You:	What did she do?
Antagonist:	[Repeated imagery mutes his ears. Digs into his chest.] Butter knife? No. Cheese knife? No, no [But considers it.].
You:	What are you doing?
Antagonist:	[Unblinking.] Pocket knife? No. Bread knife? No. Carving knife? Paring knife? Boning knife? No, no, no! Where did I put it? [Something echoing resonates. There is an awakening of menace involved.] There it is.

You: [Looks at *Dialogue* and chooses not to accept this. *Dialogue's*
                mouth is unstitched.]

Antagonist: [Without joints.] So I leave the house after
                arguing with her. She
                found missing pills and I
                said, "I didn't." And I don't know
                if I can, but I left, and she was
                crying and yelling. My dad comes
                and tells her that it is hers, so she
                is domestically running to the
                kitchen and grabs [Reaches into his
                breast cavity.]
                this [Pulls out the cleaver
                grin.] and [Grabs *Dialogue*,
                Dialogue and *Antagonist* both
                screaming.] slice! [*Antagonist* sets
                Dialogue on fire with a serrated
                edge (drooling).] [In unison with the narrative.]
                She cuts, and cuts, and cuts… [This continues for a
                while. *Time* looks at the clock and leaves. *Dialogue*
                is serrated to no applause.]

You: Is this the climax?

Antagonist: It's the truth.

                                                        Exit *You.*

Act II: [*A Canvas in Arms.*]

Justin, as an Epilogue:

Justin (*as a beginning*):

Mom,

I think I've started a play thinking that there is a beginning somewhere in the milky subconscious of beginnings. But this letter addresses the middle where I believe everything starts. In the middle, I'm beginning to realize the importance of your *I tried to off myself Justin*. And then you ask, middling my beginning, if I resent you. Mom, at this point in the play, the play begins to realize its botched 'offing' of self with a cleaver and to its dismay, it doesn't end. It attempts an exit, realizing that it is only at the middle of some absurdist plot where all the characters form to bear witness, burning their masking instruments, mimicking the play's silent shaking. The play turns its wrists over, its contents spilling onto the floor, seeing the written scribe trying to digest this sequence of events, resenting but also saying 'stop' with every courtesy that language provides. I don't know what happens next, but in this play I want to tell you what I can't write about without betraying my poetics (as *Vices*). I want to articulate using every brittle shade of sound that I carry with my beginning. I am under this impression. This play is no different.

Grandma, in an Act of Remorse, Comes to Savor

[*Mombo* attempts proclivity, which is misunderstood to mean saving. Instead, there is understanding with herself, and only herself. She is hopeful that her actions translate to something legible, but she unconvincingly issues her parting words to *Dialogue.* She will rescue the scene and then make the scene about herself. This scene wasn't supposed to, but did regardless, and she is saved. *Mombo,* reappearing, is short-dressed in collected patches of violin strings, the sound reflecting the intentions of the misinterpreted. She is misinterpreted, consequently wielding the edge of a cheese knife, creating a moment of pause within her twitching fingers.][8]

Mom: I serenely promise to regurgitate the lowest parts of the self. [*Arms* becomes out-locked in straitjackets.]

---

[8] Note to actor playing *Mombo*: You will receive only one breath.

Mombo:	Sweetie.
Mom:	I only had three choices, and I chose the one that let me be heard. [*Legs* becomes *Arms*, but the reverse is not true.]
Justin:	I don't like reciting this part. It doesn't fit.
Mombo:	Yoo hoo!
Mom:	Just look at this. [Unravels her wrists, which are made whole again. She looks perplexed.] No, this isn't what I did. No, this isn't right.
Mombo:	You know, sweetie, you should never reveal so much blood. Your kids carry that gene. I think not having kids is selfish.
Mom:	I only had three choices.
Justin:	I don't know if counting precludes honesty, but Mom, you're being dishonest. We induce counting during times of quiet.

Mombo: [She is breaking from herself directly to *Mom*.] All your father would do is drink and we would go to yoo hoo! parties like this, but he was just awful. He would show up and ruin the whole yoo hoo! evening for everyone. I would drink too, but it was hard. In those days, being a single yoo hoo! parent was tough, constantly single, but it was okay to drive home. I rode in the car with your yoo hoo! father who was just awful, but I would yoo hoo! be a single parent, so I think I understand yoo hoo! when I say your husband is a drunken yoo hoo! asshole, much like Dan in those days behind the wheel, but no, no, I need to keep my lips apart from each other for now.

Mental Ward: I exist, I do.

Mom: I don't think I'm being heard. [Reflects on the showering pieces of porcelain.]

Mental Ward: [Fingers of divination cauterize *Mental Ward's* eyelids for salt.] We should be reaching a common dialogue soon.

Mom: I serenely promise not to recite my children to this.

Mombo:	[Counting backward.] He drinks too much. He drinks too much. He drinks too much.
Mental Ward:	Who?
Mombo:	My ex-husband, son-in-law, the papal prime minister, my gynecologist, pastoral poets, but being a single parent, [*sneezes*] I mean really selfish not to have kids. But it's hard.
Mom:	Hello?

Enter an impatient *Godot.*

Godot:	Hello?
Mental Ward:	No, not yet.

[*Mental Ward* chases *Godot* offstage.]

Mombo: [Swallows a trumpet mute.] You know, I've seen alcoholism before. [With some assurance from *The Audience*.] Dan was an alcoholic.

[*Justin* unwraps the propensity for most things incoherent and audible.]

Mombo: [Finds herself driving.] It's hard living with someone like that, and that's why [Takes a sip.] I think it's selfish not to have kids.

Mental Ward: [Opens the stomach so that all characters may enter.] I want to bear you.

Justin: Mom?

[*Mom* gnaws at her wrists and ingests the clumping of her body. There is a whisper between the transitions from digestion to skin. *Mom* dies again and *Mental Ward* is born from her.]

Mother, as a Spilling

She paints
a canvas, and she's
bleeding
so my mother is
soothed, but spills
her words,
and this
is a depiction
without form or
an understanding.

Enter *Attempted Song to Commemorate the Occasion.*

Bleeding becomes
a numeration—
drops of her painted
pigment strokes
a knifed body as direct
method, but tarnishes
an indirect motion.

Enter *Re-Enactment of Soliloquy.*

So she shrivels
back to consciousness,
exposing muscle, bone,
and the rest
of the rooms within
the broken music
spilled that night.

Exit *Sleeping State of Tender.*

[Stage Theory 5]

[*Mental Ward* opens to reveal]:

Complementarity (as *Physics*):   Holds
objects governed
by quantum
measures, giving
results that depend
inherently upon
the type of device
used, and must
necessarily be described
in classical
mechanical terms.

***Justin*, as an Epilogue:**

Justin (*as a beginning*):

Mom,

I do feel guilty because I see you after and I can't count how many times you show me your scar thinking that I'll learn something from it. I've learned to leave all characters digested in the semi-solids of dialogue. Maybe this is an expression of an impulse.

[*Mom* Hacks Away at Herself, While We Watch]

Justin: Look, she's glowing.

Mombo: [Dictates the cutting.] Yoo hoo! [Winding the phonograph.] Sweetie, let me take a picture.

Act 1:   How should I interpret this?

Ghost: As a ghost.

Mental Ward: I'm ready. I think it's time.

Justin: Is this what happened?

Mombo: Tilt your chin [***hiccups***] runs in our family.

Act 1:   I will now take shape as a sonnet! [Wilts
the syllables required for untendoned
stage direction, but there is narration
of apologies forming underneath
the forms shaping the son's stomach lining.
There is a moment of panic until
the skinned body walks across the blue swept,
infecting *Act 1* as an infection
of form. This shape I held, understanding
the womb, the stomach lining hacked away,
a cleaver serrates the syllabic count.
I don't know how to say this, but she {ends}
commits herself to ten less syllables,
14 lines, and *Act 1* is not enough.]

Justin: [Genetics.] Yoo hoo! I've made an unscripted sonnet.

Mental Ward: I'm ready.

Justin: [Strand 2 of genetics.] [***hiccups, sneezes, and then spills***] Don't spill on the sonnet!

[*Mental Ward* births *Ghost*.]

Justin: [Stringed frets.] Oh no.

[The phonograph spits out a picture, which grows into a blurred object.]

Ghost: [Solidifies as a comforting presence.] I'm leaving.

Exit *Birdcage Forgetting It's Not a Lantern*.

***Justin*, as an Epilogue:**

Justin (*as a beginning*):

Mom,

You used a cleaver, but during the beginning of this project, I truly doubted that cleavers held the vindictiveness of suicide. As the image passes of you holding such an impossible object, staring down at your wrists with such distrust, I'm left with your confirmation as a faint laugh that *You're not supposed to cut with a cleaver* as you try to. But if you had used another knife, and cut in a different direction, you would be in a different state of dead, and this wouldn't be a play about botched suicide, knives, living scars, psych wards, and my grandmother. It would then be a play about a different mourning—one where your body forgets what it once held on to, thirsting away for cleavers.

Intermission: *Pathos* Takes a Look at *Back-Stage* Undressing

Cupboard: What am I doing here? This isn't where cupboards are meant. [Notices that *Curtains* are in the throes of fire, but no one else seems to care.]

Heart: I brought you here.

Cupboard: Why?

Heart: Because the play is stale.

Cupboard: Since when?

Heart: Since conception.

Cupboard: Gross.

Heart: [Turns his attention to *Stage* where *Dialogue* is wrapped in a blanket of pus and nods.] Gross.

Cupboard: I'll be leaving now. [Turns away and makes for the exit (stage left).]

[*Heart* grabs *Cupboard*, shaking, blowing rope, flower petals, heads, the scent echoing after *you can't leave*, reattaching a space to reach into, now opening. *Heart* controls its pulse and enters, finding *Straw* inside painting a blue hymn to *Cupboard's* cornea. *Heart* notices some sewn drawings along *Cupboard's* walls depicting *Act 1* giving birth to *Chairs 1 and 2*. *Heart* continues plucking irises left in a corner.]

Heart: [After humming, *Heart* discards the petals to undress *Cupboard's* innards, finding them, staring.] You're really quite beautiful.

Cupboard: [Out of discomfort.] Tomato soup, canned oranges, legumes, pasta, oat bran, flour petals, sour eggs, vegetable oil, leftover meatloaf, hot dog buns, kale, hard baguettes, ice trays, ladyfingers, Ziploc bags, jelly, gluten-free banana bread, lactose-free soy milk, almond paste, spoiled marmalade, macaroni paintings, toothbrush, salt splinters, raspberry vinaigrette, centurion spaghetti, condensed cauliflower, do-it-yourself sausage, mystery eggplant, thumbtack substitute, citronella, peanut butter, pickled pigs' feet, canned heron, substitute chicken salad—

Heart: [Intimately lower.] This is what's best for the play.

Cupboard: What's going on? This doesn't normally happen in plays, but in poetry.

[*Heart* purrs but says nothing, knowing that it's too late.]

Enter *Mombo* breaking through, wearing *The Audience* in place of *Boa*.

Mombo: [Alleges *Sicilians* to *Incest*. *The Audience* is in a state of shawls.] I've read somewhere that Sicily [Checks her notes.] was conquered by the Moors, after being uprooted in North Africa. So the pre-Moorish Sicilians were conquered and became post-Moorish Sicilians with their siblings, thus explaining this play's heritage. My son-in-law is a Moorish sister with children, and that's why Sicilians are [*hiccups*] really selfish not to have kids. [Takes a cosmetic sip.]

Cupboard: [Staring inwardly.] She's terrible.

Heart: [Withholding a sheep in the mouth.] She's our Mentor.

[Out of *Cupboard*.] Enter *Aeneas*.

Aeneas:	I opened the Gate of Ivory.
Cupboard:	[Blushes a corset crimson.] I must have been dreaming.
Aeneas:	[Notices the dripping depictions of corsets.] I must have picked the wrong gate.
Heart:	[Still inside.] Why are you here?
Aeneas:	Stoicism.
Heart:	[Sharp.] Oh no, I think he's Italian!
Mombo:	[Pounces.] You look like my son-in-law.
Aeneas:	Madam, I can assure you I do not have time for this. I must be the founder of—
Mombo:	Sicily.
Aeneas:	No, wench, Rome.
Mombo:	Yoo hoo! The Pope founded Rome, sweetie.
Aeneas:	[Draws a good wind to travel.] I really don't have time for this.
Mombo:	[Sinks the vessel holding safe passage.] I was just telling that fine piece of cabinetry over there about Sicilian love affairs. That is why you all carry such terrible tempers.
Aeneas:	The gods dictate that I must spurn all love in order to fulfill my duty.

[Cue *Molly Bloom* on a burning pyre, orchestrating her swan song.]

Molly Bloom:	Yes.

Mombo:	[As the *Gate of Horn*.] I hope you don't drink, sweetie. My ex-husband was a drinker, and all he founded was depression.
Aeneas:	The gods dictate that I spurn ambrosia in order to found the Romans.
Mombo:	I'm my daughter's caretaker.

Enter *The Underworld*.

Underworld:	[As the passageway for slitting.] Aeneas, come back.
Aeneas:	[Seeing the ghost of his father.] How?
Underworld:	By re-enacting the scene between Odysseus, Circe, Calypso, and the Misinterpreted Cupboard of Troy.

Aeneas: [Lays a pentagram of myrrh inside himself and begins toward *Mombo,* deaf to the meaning of his following words.] You are your daughter's caretaker.

[*Mombo* knots in the seasons, creating turquoise.]

Aeneas: [With the last spectered syllable.] You are your daughter's caretaker.

[*Mombo* opens the slit to the next scene.]

Exit *Aeneas* through *Mombo.*

[*Aeneas* finds himself in a kitchen as *Mom* draws the pigments out of herself. This is his second time witnessing the death of a literary love figure.]

Mombo: [Peeks through an aperture and then after, unsulfurs a cigarette
              into *Cupboard*, humming *Straw's* forgotten blue hymn.] Yoo
              hoo! Heart, sweetie, bring me a scale.

                      Enter *Heart* with a balance scale from out of *Cupboard*.

Mombo: [Blindfolds herself using her fingers and sits on the 'Against'
              weighing pan. She continues humming.] No, the play will
              continue.

                      Enter *Audience's Monologue* (the whisperings of the few).

Audience: No! The play must die. The play must die. The play must
              [Dies.].

      [*Mombo* goes off to look through the aperture again.]

Heart: [Alone with *Cupboard*.] She takes care of her after she does that
              to herself.

Cupboard: Why a cleaver though?

Heart: [Again, inside and shut.] She made a mistake.

[Stage Theory 6]

[*Mental Ward* opens to reveal]:

Young's Slit Experiment: A creation story in which *Young* steps forward, looks inward, ripples *Reflection*, and precedes *Essence*. In this inward setting, he decides to create matter from the body of two slits for *Light*[9] to wave. *Light* passes through the slits. The resulting naked intimacy is observed and recorded behind a hiding curtain camouflaged in ink, where *Reflection* lies blank and wordless. A sweaty, anatomical *Light* produces bright and dark bands, straining for existence, logic, and chaos until uncomfortably observed. The results are recorded. *Light* pools on the floor, trying to escape from this creation story. *Young*, afraid of his creation, pokes and prods the scientific reasoning holding *Light* to shape, like any other marshmallow campfire scene. Other lyrical phantoms of the written word take part, searching for perspective. *Young* says something distant, and suddenly *Fire* burns out. Every phantom is stranded. *Reality* cuts all umbilical ties with *Young*, now apologizing, grasping for reason. The results are recorded. *Young* wakes up, never really sleeping, flailing wings that are not wings, nor his, giving names to objects whispered in his ear, substituting his atoms for words, clinging to space as a grounding element, crawling up blinking walls, then looking, blinking, then gone. *Light* is left behind, shaping to the particles comprising *Subconscious*, no longer noticed. This dark singularity is introduced as *Universe*, illuminating a *Cloaked Epiphany*, who bears all for no one to see.

Cloaked Epiphany: Philosophical thinking begins with the human subject—not merely the thinking subject, but the acting, feeling, living human character.

---

[9] The personification of the idea that there is no meaning to be found in the world beyond what meaning we give to it.

Young descends further into himself, and from the remaining embers heaving from a carbon element, finds a precise glass cylinder tangled in dirt, which he names *Beaker*. He resumes his creation story, regaining some form of compositional control, placing measurements of *Bunsen Burner* and *Kafka* within *Beaker*. *Young* begins chanting, "I acknowledge that philosophical creation begins with the human subject." The collected literary phantoms begin chanting with *Young*, incorporating a Freudian minor scale, each decibel introducing a new taste to what is about to transpire. *Fire* is brought to a boil.

An oxygenated glowing circle forms over *Beaker's* head, now arms open, trembling from the formation of an inner-anatomy phenomenon. *Beaker* opens his mouth, and *World* crawls out, dawning. The literary phantoms are brought to the birthing scene swaddled in applause. *World* takes its first steps towards a sweetly discarded *Light*, while a fragile *Beaker* is left to play with a sullen *Indifference*. *Fire* opens. *Light*, now the existential muse, plants a numerical value for order within *Fire*, damp from breastfeeding a sunken *Universe*.

Young, unhappy with this creation story, looks around and discovers that *Reason* does not exist. For example, *World* grows up, no longer governed by laws of gravity, and begins an affair with *Subconscious*, who once again takes the strings away from *Young*. Seeing at his own hands for the first time how truly misplaced he is within himself, *Young* says "Hello," trying to exit. But *Light* hangs over his shoulder, revealing more than words, smiling a faint, meaningless smile, and opens a seven-day resting casket that brings a new sense to the body: disorientation. *Young* considers it, feeling helpless.

Forgotten, *Reflection* scribbles notes from behind the likewise forgotten *Curtain*, and after, wakes up one morning, vulnerable to the changes surrounding him. Maybe in Sanskrit, *Young* will find *Kafka* reading—

Stage Theory 6: *Reflection's* Memoirs.

[*Because of the world's absurdity, at any point in time, anything can happen to anyone, and a tragic event could plummet someone into direct confrontation with* **The Absurd**.] [The body languages onto paper.]

> Subtract from each character [stop]
> morality [stop] existence [stop] this awakening
> [stop] a weakening pass [stop] at phrase [stop]
> emerging footsteps from behind [stop] conscious
> [stop] but breathing [stop] further
> away from [stop] *To Young, my reflection* [stop]
> a result that is [stop]
> not extraordinary [stop] leaving [stop]
> or remarkable [stop]
> fellow box [stop] taken by waves
> [stop] a cat inside [stop]
> swept under current [stop] by dripping
> light [stop] possibly everything [stop]
> slits [stop] I am creating [stop]
> nothing at all [stop]

[*Finding himself persevering through language for the first time,* **Reflection** *is taken by* **Camus** *in the* **Stocks of Absurdity** *to a place where he is put in perpetual danger of having everything meaningful break down. But before exiting through stage direction:*]

Camus: [Before a gloating, scarlet lettered *Myth of Sisyphus*.] The possibility of suicide makes all humans existentialists.

When She Opens

My mother, she—
       Botches her death in the beginning.

My mother, she—   [cuts]
          tonic water sobriety
          chamber music dialogue
          intravenous glue marrow
          milk suckling
          narrative of blood streams
          replenished scab nudity
          umbilical implications
          non-foreskinned wrists
          all language contained in dialogue
          words that call her "my mother, she—"
          the names before "Justin"
          seven days spent creating
          Your mother had a breaking
          the grief I nourish
          I don't know how to tell you this
          the mouth that forms first
          my mother, and her many bodies.

My mother, she—
       Is brought back from blood and remembers that I was fed
       pulped taro root as a child. That is why these words—
       small, stunted, and still born—continue
       to grow as an act of waking.

[*Mom* Splices Her *Anatomy*]

There's a certain amount of entropy involved
when two related bodies attempt an understanding.
But there are also actions taken that translate
to moderate resemblances. If only I knew
what motivates the body to move. But movement can
lead to applications of the self, and there is venom
in my understanding, there is movement that holds still.

I cannot undertake what symbols and shapes calcify,
these words stripped of bone, and other signs
of clawing. My mother broke herself, and reformed as
not my mother, in terms of herself, and my body was not
touched, but shattered as a piece of torn cloth,
not worn, not worn repeated, but I'm clawing.

My mother took a butcher's knife, and after ridding herself
of pores and other patterns of decay, she called the knife's edge,
rehearsed it into my brother, and placed it inside the right-handed
flaps covered with palm. *This is yours now.*
I give this a new name, and it is yours.
What I didn't want. What holds
without skin. What wilted
as my new belonging.

[Stage Theory 7]

[*Mental Ward* opens to reveal]:

Double-Slit Experiment[10]:

a demonstration that matter and energy can display the fundamentally probabilistic nature of repeating		natural repetition probability passes the fundamental energy displaying *Audience* as matter and more on stage of a demonstration phenomena

(behind the curtain);

a result
unexpected if slits
consisted strictly
absorbed,
as though discrete
photons.

---

[10] See *Interference Experiment.*

Enter *The* [Silver-Tongued] *Devil in Plaid*

[*The Devil in Plaid* cuts a hole in *Justin's* navel, and forms a contract with *Suicide*, using *Justin's* skin as leverage. This occurs so that *The Audience* knows what is at stake. For a brief moment, there is no mention of souls or admonishment; instead, the setting of the play is appreciated for all its quirks and dysfunctional personality. *Justin's* skin is put on display, ticking away until the conclusion is submerged. *The Devil in Plaid* drinks a glass of warm milk from *Justin's* skin and forms social circles of Hell using all the lost souls of *The Audience*. *Suicide* casts a lake of frozen fire onto *Stage* and chills the cold, creeping into the narration. *The Conclusion* eats away at *Dante*, but *Dante* is miscast as *Hermes the underdressed, misunderstood messenger of clarity*. What remains as *Justin* prophesies *Virgil*, and so *Virgil* is forced into labor. *Virgil* births a new narrative of Hell. Everything is bleached to ashes; consequently, *Mother* is awakened with a sprouted *Mombo* as a growth on her shoulder. *Justin* drinks the remaining milk and commits all the layers of Hell to *Mental Ward*. The remainder of the scene shall take place inside the heart of *The Devil in Plaid*.]

Devil:	Why hello my dearies!
Justin:	I think what you're doing is terrible.
Mom:	Hello?
Virgil:	I can't navigate through this place.
Dante:	Then we are all doomed!
Justin:	I think we just need to repent for a great sin.
Devil:	Sin? What's that?
Justin:	It's when you write a play to describe the inner workings of mourning.
Devil:	Oh? And what are we mourning?
Justin:	My mother.

Devil: [Points to *Mom.*] You mean her?

Justin: Yes.

Virgil: But she's moving.

Justin: Yes.

Dante: So what's the issue?

Justin: She—

Mombo: Yoo hoo!

[*Justin*, satirizing the sentiment behind trances, continues to mouth the story, unhearing interruptions to the narrative.]

Mom: [Exposes her roots.] I cut myself.

Devil: Oh, that's not so bad. I forgive you.

Dante: Well, during my time suicide was a great sin.

Suicide: [Unclothed, in prenatal nudity.] I beg your pardon?

Dante: Virgil, what do I do?

  [*The Devil in Plaid* wags his finger and *Virgil* gives birth to *Ending.*]

Virgil: Dante, what do I do?

Suicide: I beg your pardon, sir!

Mombo: Yoo hoo! My ex-husband would act like this after drinking.
             Children should not have to endure alcoholism, [Reads a
             passage from *The Dialogues.*] and that's why it's really selfish
             not to have kids.

  [*The Devil in Plaid* wags his finger and *Virgil* gives birth to a litter of
  Aeneids.]

Justin: [Finishes his epileptic trance.]
             Yoo hoo, look at me
             and how I say
             "olive oil," my father is
             Italian, sweetie,
             Dan, who shall remain
             nameless in death, is my
             Cent'anni grandfather, Dante
             with juniper consummates
             poetry, my mother is
             En trance, suicide enters
             the body, skin bleeds out an
             escape, the great Roman
             laurel, I think therefore I mustn't
             veni, vidi, vici create
             in terms of line breaks and body
             parting, my mother admits in her
             lines that she isn't
             the scented candle, or the libations
             of myrrh, Syllabic Virgil, you are a
             Devil in your own words, but

I mustn't question what I am
doing, I mustn't question what I am
doing, I mustn't question
poetry from bleeding—

Mombo: Yoo—

Devil: No, that's enough.

[*The Devil in Plaid* wags his finger and *Virgil* gives birth to the teeth that ingest *Mombo's* lips with stitching.]

Mom: Justin, I'm not dead though.

Dante: I don't know if that's what he's saying.

Justin: [Can't bring himself to look.] My mother cut herself.

Virgil: Dido is spurned and impales herself.

Dante: There is a circle of Hell designated for suicide.

[A rose shatters offstage.]

Devil: [To himself.] (1st) Limbo, (2nd) lust, (3rd) gluttony, (4th) greed, (5th) anger, (6th) heresy, (7th) violence, (8th) fraud, (9th) treachery, (10th) agony, (11th) expired goldfish, (12th) Ponzi schemers, (13th) forgetfulness, (14th) Halloween costumes, (15th) paparazzi, (16th) neo-testament mediators, (17th) good scotch, (18th) those who waste it, (19th) Purgatory, (20th) unbaptized syntax errors, (21st) acronyms, (22nd) neophytes, (23rd) Etc., (24th) Acme Corp. Insta-Manifestos, (25th) Christopher Marlowe doppelgängers, (26th) bloodletting scales, (27th) minor chords, (28th) Chair 2, (29th) Godot…

Justin: [Kisses them both.] Let me grieve while my mother's living. [Begins to make a new entrance.]

Mom: Justin, the doctor gave me a cream to cover the scar.

Virgil / Dante: [Together.] Hippocrates calls it, "Ambrosia!"

Justin: [Looks up slowly.] Scars are areas of fibrous tissue, the acts that replace normal skin after injury.

[The scene fades out as a still-life painting of memory.]

Justin, as an Epilogue:

Mom: I cut across my wrist, but didn't know
you are supposed to cut the entire length
of the forearm, the palette elbow, grain
against the crux, where I would know not to
cross the climate in my wrists, bearings etched
in known pigment. I cut across my arm
offerings, and this was a mistake. The
length speaking to my shapeless scar. My verse
holding my length, left wanting across to
work the length straining my first mention of
water in its entire scope of language.
I committed an act of suicide,
and water turned against blood, against ash,
against the metal blade within myself.

Justin: [As a beginning.] Mom, I think I grow smaller in my sleep.

[Stage Theory 8]

End.

[*Mental Ward* opens to reveal]:

Chthonic White Space:

is the technical adjective
measured by
how perfectly a scene
can cancel
destructive
interference relationships

between   characters   [between]

observed

at different

[Enter *Character.*]   moments on   [Exit *Character.*]
----
stage.

Final Act in Unspoken Chords

Dream: I am wearing breath.

Mom: What an odd thing to say.

Dream: Oh, it's you!

Mom: How do you know?

Dream: Are you kidding? Everyone knows.

Mom: That doesn't answer my question.

Dream: We are all created for the sole purpose of conveying your actions.

Mom: [Cuts her wrists using the breath worn.] I just cut myself.

Dream: Are you going to be okay?

Mom: I think so.

Sonnet: Hello.

Dream: [Undergoes a purification of veins.] Oh lovely! It's you!

Mom: I'm alive though.

Sonnet: [Vapors.] That's not the point!

[For the sake of an alternate play, *Sonnet* embodies a blade that can ensure that *Mom* enters a more certain state of death. However, *Justin* cannot write an alternate play, as *Mom* cannot kill herself.]

                                                     Enter *The Unspoken Poem.*

The Unspoken Poem: [Written to a gathered quiet *Chorus.*]

                      …clarity stretched

                      lineless, feeding

                      under silk

                      clotting nightscapes,

                      enveloped in

                      pouring moments

                      of loss, my words

                      as image, the sentence

                      miraged as a mirage,

                      spilled water,

                      more intimate

                      flooding,

                      or dialect without

                      scent paints back

                      the image

                      of what now holds

                      where our veins place

                      our figments

                      beyond melody.

                                       The Unspoken Poem bows and exits.

[An Alternate Play *en scène*]

Justin: My mom is dead.

Dream: Oh? How did she die?

Justin: Suicide.

Suicide: Yes?

Sonnet: [As *The Omnipotent*.] That's terrible.

Closure: May I enter?

Mom: [Breaking away from this improvised script.] I'm not dead. I can never take back what I did, but at least I'm still alive.

Justin: [Unmasked as *Sonnet*.] You're alive, but you cut your wrist with a cleaver. You bled all over the floor, wanting to die. I have to look at you, and every time, you are dead.

[*Mom* cuts the umbilical prose.]

Mom: Do you forgive me?

[*Justin* takes a cleaver.]

Justin: I'm about to do something terrible.

Dream: [As an aside.] Not to be spiteful, I hope.

[*Justin* takes a cleaver.]

Dream: [As an aside.] Either way, I no longer want to take part in this.

[*Justin* takes a cleaver. *Family* is assembled. *Justin* slashes his wrists until bone on bone is revealed, and cartilage pours out, marrow creates inkblots, and a venoming of color sprays onto *Mom's* face. *Family* faints as an aside. *Justin* splits his wrist from ligament and shoves the handed-bulb into *Mom's* flickering throat, finger by finger. *Justin* acknowledges the fruits spoiled. There is no movement towards speech. *Justin* bleeds out and *Mom* bleeds out but both characters are connected only by their undying.]

Mom: [In a forgotten Gaelic.] No one would listen to me.

Justin: [Writes.] You didn't die, but you took action toward ending our bonded speech.

Mom: I don't know what to say.

[There is a growing, exponential pause. *Justin*, dripping, looks into his mother and traces the lineage of her adoptive scarring with the dull end of the cleaver. He touches her hand with his.]

Justin: [After struggling, finds it.] I know.

[*Justin* kisses her cheek, causing an *Exeunt All.*]

Exeunt *All.* Enter *Dialogue.*

[*Dialogue* emerges from the letter left behind in *Act I*, and opens revealing *Godot as Watercolor Closure.*]

Godot: [To *The Audience* leaning against a tree, peeling a nourished tangerine.] Hello.

To my mother who is brought back.

[*Justin* reads to *The Audience* in place of *Pantoum 2*.]

This is the first line that draws open my mother's quartered note body.
This is the first line that calls my being into my mother.
This is the first line that places versed blood into an hourglass.
This line botches its commitment to suicide, leaking into folded grief.

My mother is the first line to botch existing,
insufficiently dead, and consequently mistreated as a line break.
She commits to her suicidal memory, folding skin to language,
becoming my mother, who cuts the first line I cannot finish.

She is insufficiently dead; a maternal postmortem ward
of remains left behind by my moving mother.
The remnant body of the second line births the first line,
botching the order of suicide, spilling my mother.

My mother moves within this line, drawing remaining blood,
shaping her death, veins and tongues spilled in immersion,
and then the lisping knives re-emerge through the second line of wrists,
bleeding my self-inflicted mother to voweled breath.

Veined chords play an obsession with her tongue, spilling shapeless
and dissonant across soundless bleeding and snapped skin.
These open slits of syllables call to her living body
deeply red; exposure of my unfleshed mother's resuscitation.

My mother's scarred words evoke snapped skin chimes:
Justin, you might not forgive me, repeated through resuscitated hearts.
The first line reimagines the death of the following line—
The last line that plucks away at my mother's body.

Epigraph:

Mental Ward: [All skin caked in seeds.]
                 Holding shape to syntax
                 lips knives to prayers
                 of skinned constriction;
                 there are words inside me.

Justin Limoli works with bonsai and orchids as a writer and horticulturist. He lives in Maui, Hawaii.

I want these words to radiate the warmth I feel for you Joshua Young, Tyler Crumrine, Jill Magi, Maureen Seaton, my peers, and the faculty at Columbia College Chicago. Without your encouragement, guidance, and patience, this work would never have blemished these pages. I am sending out into the world a work that bears your markings (see how they glow?) knowing that I will cherish it close to my heart. You have given me this gift, so thank you thank you thank you.

Thank you also Kevin Killian and Kris Saknussemm (and the two muses above) for taking *Bloodletting* to heart, letting it resonate, and articulating the most positive reviews I have ever received. And to David Watt for depicting what took me two years and 75 pages in a single image.

I must also express a more formal thank you to Jack Spicer, Shakespeare, Epic Poetry, Lyrical Plays, the impulse to express our impossible objects, *The Muse*, all the notes that cling to these strings, my characters, *The Audience*, and time.

Most importantly, I want to thank my mother, whom I love with everything. I hope I express that enough, that I love you with everything.